THE TRUTH ABOUT
ELEPHANTS

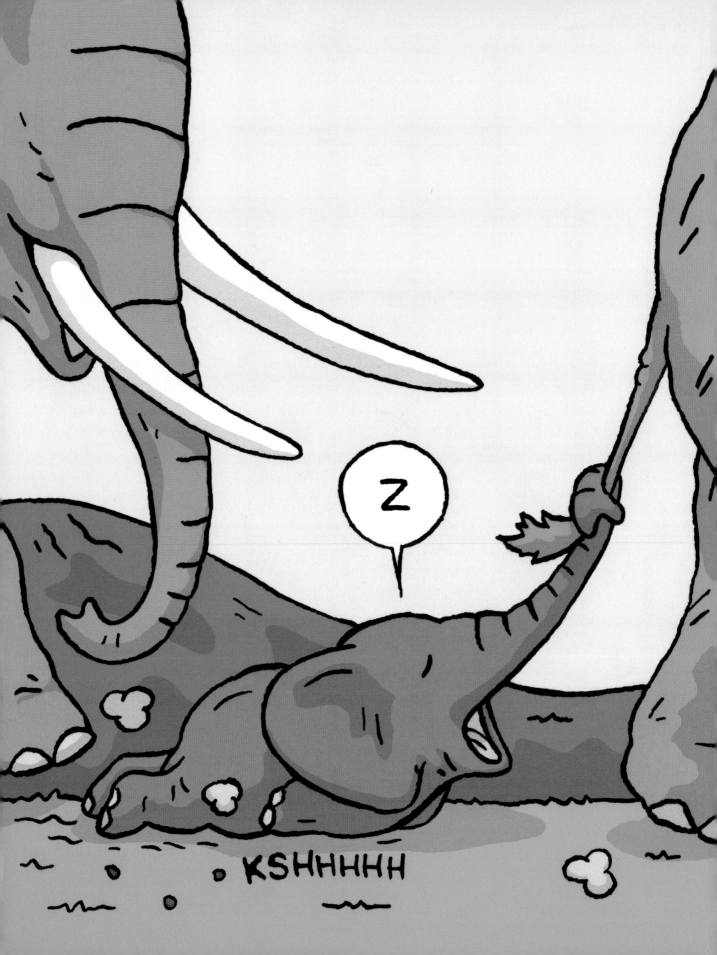

THE TRUTH ABOUT ELEPHANTS

Maxwell Eaton III

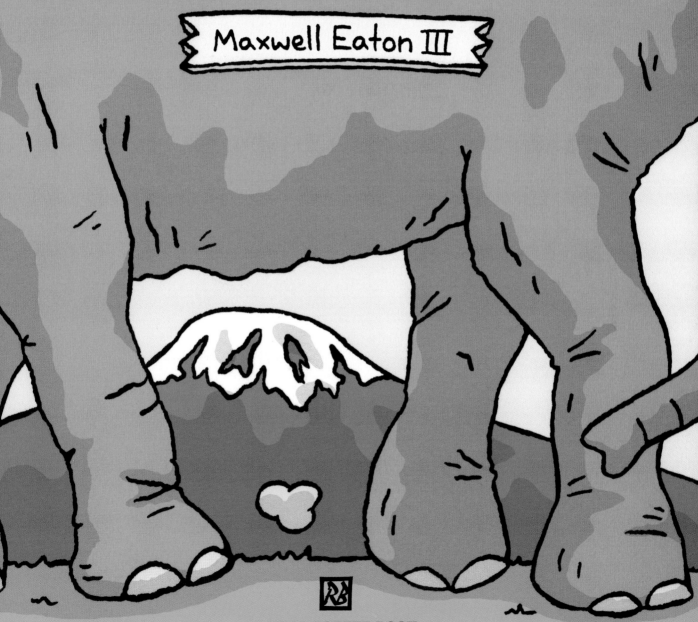

A NEAL PORTER BOOK
ROARING BROOK PRESS
NEW YORK

Published by Roaring Brook Press
Roaring Brook Press is a division of Holtzbrinck
Publishing Holdings Limited Partnership
175 Fifth Avenue, New York, NY 10010
The art for this book was created using pen and ink with digital coloring.
mackids.com

ISBN: 978-1-62672-669-7
Library of Congress Control Number: 2018935641

Our books may be purchased in bulk for promotional, educational, or business use. Please
contact your local bookseller or the Macmillan Corporate and Premium Sales Department at
(800) 221-7945 ext. 5442 or by e-mail at MacmillanSpecialMarkets@macmillan.com.

First edition, 2018
Book design by Jennifer Browne

Printed in China by Shaoguan Fortune Creative Industries Co. Ltd.,
Shaoguan, Guangdong Province

1   3   5   7   9   10   8   6   4   2

Here comes an elephant.

Elephants are the largest animals on land.

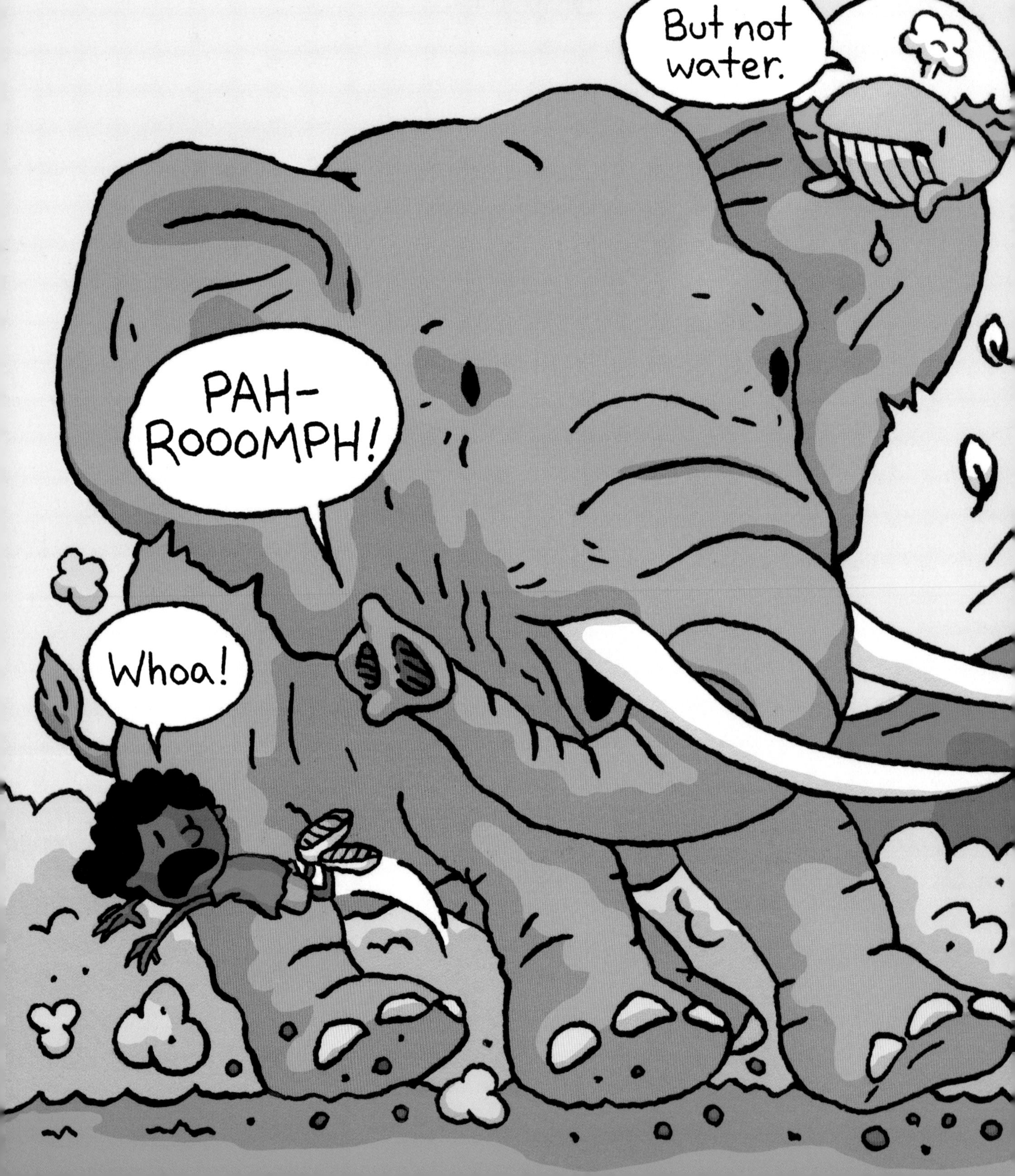

AFRICAN SAVANNA ELEPHANT (BULL)
LENGTH: 24 FT.
HEIGHT: 11 FT.
WEIGHT: 11,000 LBS.
LIVES 60 YEARS OR LONGER!
Party size.
ELEPHANT WORDS
COW: ADULT FEMALE
BULL: ADULT MALE
CALF: YOUNG ELEPHANT
Ah!
Show-off.
Hmph.
KERSH!
White rhinoceros: 5,000 lbs.
Common hippopotamus: 7,000 lbs.

Elephants evolved over millions of years with similar (now extinct) animals.

Today there are two main types of elephant. They are alike in most ways, but have a few small differences.

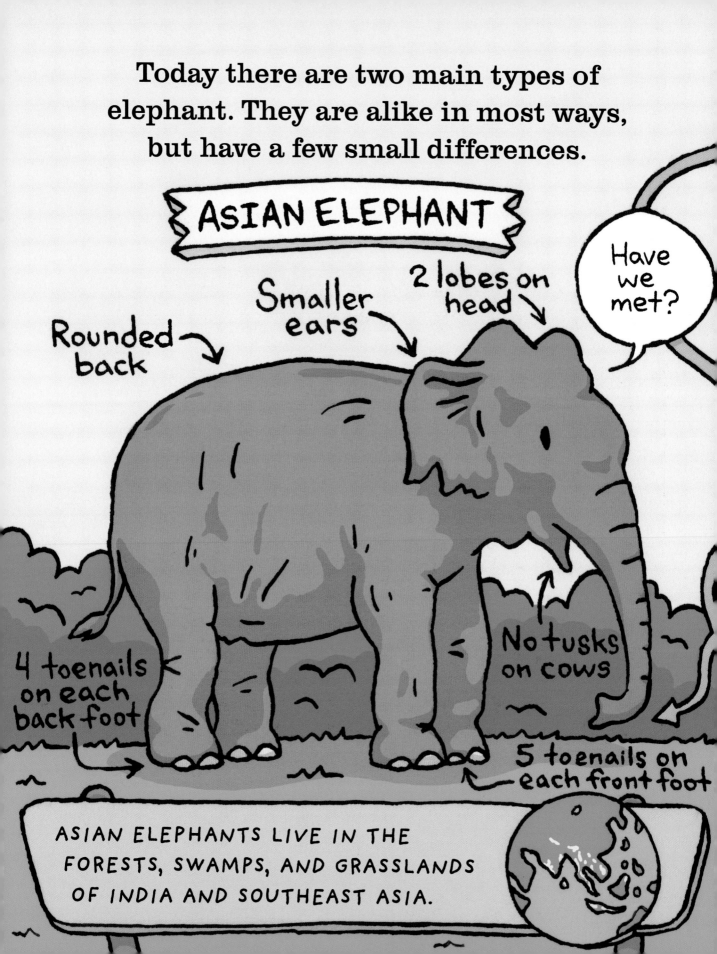

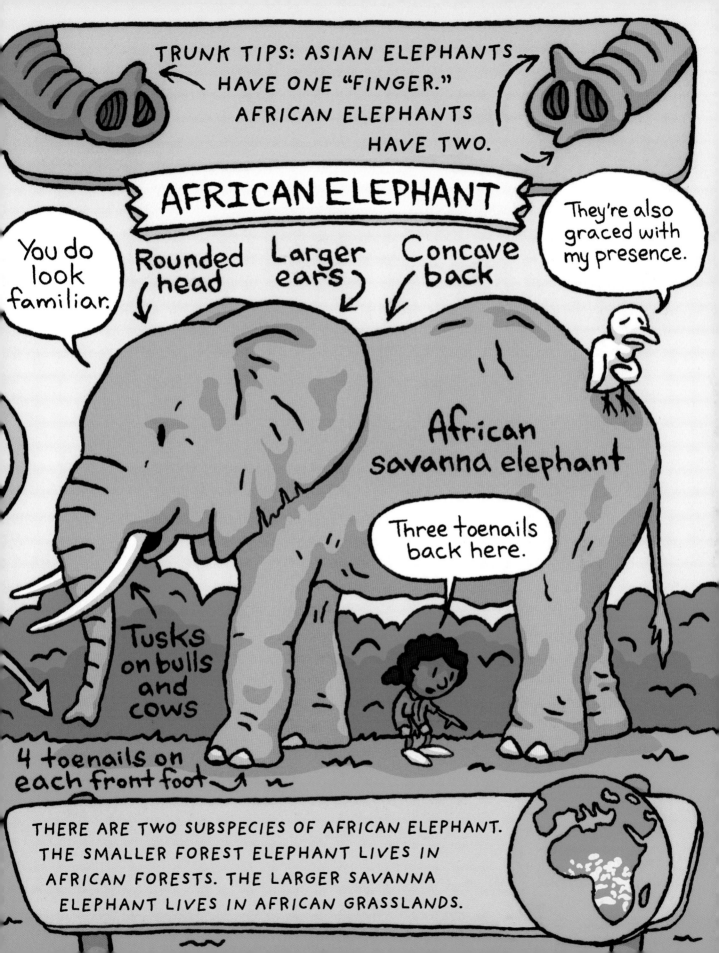

Elephants have extended noses called trunks.
Trunks are used for just about everything.

Elephants' teeth are also unique. Long tusks are used to dig for roots, scrape bark from trees, and defend against predators.

ELEPHANTS' TUSKS NEVER STOP GROWING. THE OLDER THE ELEPHANT, THE BIGGER THE TUSKS!

Elephants chew their food with four gigantic molars. Those molars are eventually worn down, and a new set comes in from behind and pushes out the old teeth.

Elephants are herbivores. That means they eat only plants. When the weather is rainy, they choose mostly grass, leaves, roots, and fruits.

When it's dry, they eat twigs, shrubs, and bark. A large elephant may even push over an entire tree for an easier meal.

Elephants usually live in herds made up of six to twelve family members—one grandmother, her adult daughters, and their young female and male calves.

Along with trumpeting, elephants make low-pitched rumbling growls that sound like enormous cats purring.

When a herd of elephants senses danger, they huddle together, with the calves hiding between the adults' legs.

The matriarch will stand tall, spread her ears, trumpet, and even rip up and throw a bush at the intruder. This usually does the trick, but when it doesn't . . .

Elephants are wary of tigers, crocodiles, lions, and hyenas, but their biggest threat wears shoes.

Humans hunt elephants for their tusks.

Horses?

I would prefer they did not.

They clear forests of trees and plants.

This seems unreasonable.

Their houses creep into elephant habitats.

And they cut up the land with roads.

The threats are enormous, but you can begin to help by reading about elephants, and then teaching others and speaking out.